W9-CUD-196

U.S.A. TRAVEL GUIDES

IDAHO

BY ANN HEINRICHS • ILLUSTRATED BY MATT KANIA

The Child's World®
childsworld.com

Published by The Child's World®
1980 Lookout Drive • Mankato, MN 56003-1705
800-599-READ • www.childsworld.com

Photo Credits

Photographs ©: Shutterstock Images, cover, 1, 31,
37 (bottom); Nan Palmero CC2.0, 7; Kyle Brutke/
iStockphoto, 8; Tom Reichner/Shutterstock Images, 11;
Gregory Johnston/Shutterstock Images, 12; Bureau of
Land Management Idaho, 15; Tucker James/Shutterstock
Images, 16; George Sheldon/Shutterstock Images, 19;
Zvonimir Atletic/Shutterstock Images, 20; D Guisinger
CC2.0, 23; Bob Wick/Bureau of Land Management
- California, 24; Zechariah Judy CC2.0, 27; Everett
Historical/Shutterstock Images, 28; Barbara Tripp/
Shutterstock Images, 32; Paul Vinten/Shutterstock Images,
35; Atlas Pix/Shutterstock Images, 37 (top)

ISBN 9781503819528
LCCN 2016961128

Printing

Printed in the United States of America
PA02334

Ann Heinrichs is the author
of more than 100 books
for children and young
adults. She has also enjoyed
successful careers as a
children's book editor and
an advertising copywriter.
Ann grew up in Fort Smith,
Arkansas, and lives in
Chicago, Illinois.

About the Author
Ann Heinrichs

Matt Kania loves maps and, as a
kid, dreamed of making them. In
school he studied geography and
cartography, and today he makes
maps for a living. Matt's favorite
thing about drawing maps is
learning about the places they
represent. Many of the maps
he has created can be found in
books, magazines, videos, Web
sites, and public places.

About the
Map Illustrator
Matt Kania

On the cover: Sun Valley is a favorite spot for skiers.

OUR IDAHO TRIP

Are you ready for a great adventure? Then hop aboard for a trip through Idaho!

You'll meet fur trappers and mountain men. You'll take a rough ride on a wild river. You'll see moose, mountain goats, and beavers. You'll go deep down into a silver mine. And you'll fall into a pit of mashed potatoes!

Does this sound like your kind of fun? Then take your seat and buckle up. We're off to tour Idaho!

WELCOME TO
IDAHO

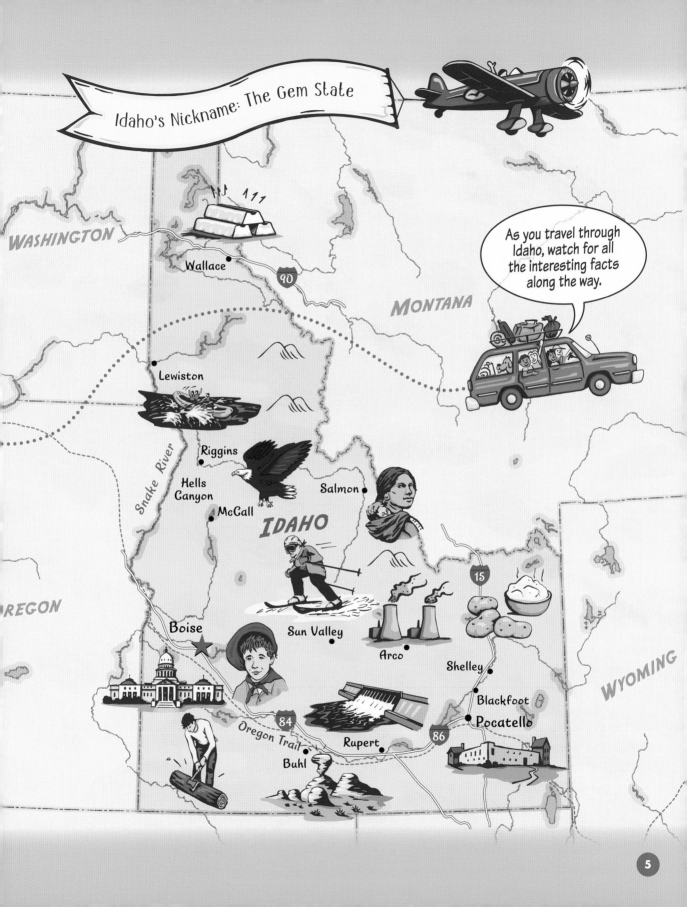

Yellowstone National Park reaches into eastern Idaho. Most of this park is in Wyoming.

Lowest Temperature: Island Park Dam January 18, 1943 -60°F (-51°C)

Highest Temperature: Orofino July 28, 1934 118°F (48°C)

Look at those bighorn sheep on the mountainside! How do they jump from rock to rock without falling?

Canada borders Idaho to the north. Washington and Oregon lie to the west. Montana and Wyoming are on the east. Nevada and Utah are south of Idaho.

HIGHEST AND LOWEST POINTS
Highest: Borah Peak at 12,662 feet (3,859 m)
Lowest: Snake River at Lewiston at 710 feet (216 m)

Lake Pend Oreille is Idaho's largest lake. It's in the Panhandle.

Idaho's northernmost area is a narrow piece of land. It's called the Panhandle.

Hells Canyon is the deepest canyon in North America. It's deeper than Arizona's Grand Canyon.

CANADA
WASHINGTON
Panhandle
Lake Pend Oreille
MONTANA
Rocky Mountains
Orofino
Lewiston
OREGON
Snake River
Hells Canyon
Borah Peak
Island Park Dam
Yellowstone National Park
WYOMING

BOATING THROUGH HELLS CANYON

Whee! The waters rush and swirl around you. Curious animals watch from the riverbanks. Towering peaks rise overhead. You're racing through Hells Canyon! It's a deep **gorge** on the Snake River.

The Snake River is Idaho's major river. It crosses the southern part of the state. Then it forms part of the western border. That's where Hells Canyon is. The fields in the river plain are very fertile. They receive irrigation water from the river.

The Rocky Mountains cover northern and central Idaho. These rugged mountains are wild and beautiful. Many of them have snowcapped peaks all year long. Some of Idaho's wilderness areas have no roads.

Grab a raft and head through Hells Canyon!

ROCKS, CAVES, AND WATERFALLS

The giant rock looms high overhead. It weighs as much as ten elephants! But it balances on just a tiny base. It's the world-famous Balanced Rock near Buhl. The City of Rocks is another rocky wonder. This jumble of granite is near Almo. Its rocks are worn into many strange shapes.

Idaho also has hundreds of underground caves. The caves north of Shoshone are known as the Shoshone Ice caves. Their icy walls sparkle.

Lots of waterfalls tumble down Idaho's rocky cliffs. Shoshone Falls is on the Snake River near Twin Falls. Shoshone Native Americans call it "hurling waters leaping."

The Balanced Rock in Idaho is a natural wonder.

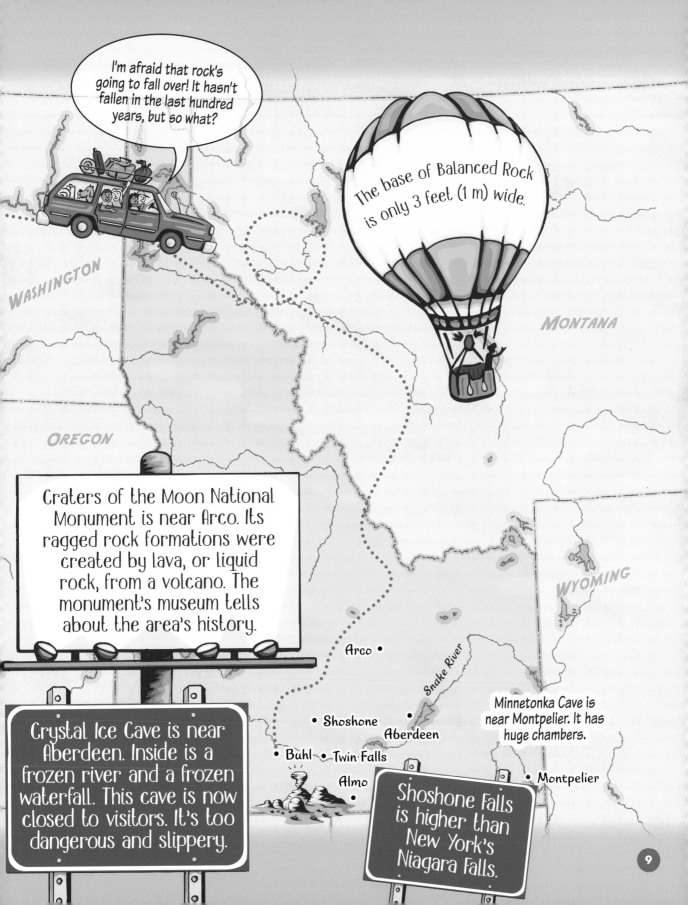

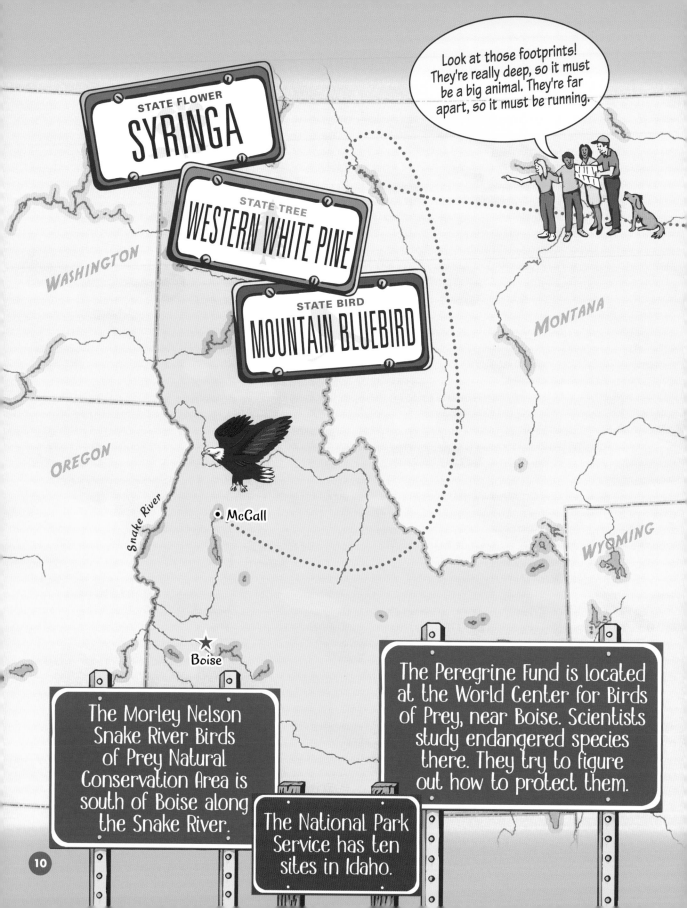

WATCHING WILDLIFE IN PAYETTE NATIONAL FOREST

Listen for a high-pitched "eep!" sound. It's made by a rabbit-like animal called a pika. Look high on the rocky cliffs. You'll see mountain goats with nimble feet. Pass by a lake. Moose are standing knee-deep in the water. Beavers and salmon are swimming nearby.

You're wandering through Payette National Forest. It's in west central Idaho near McCall. This region has few people. That makes it a great home for wildlife.

Bird-watchers find a lot to watch in Idaho. Eagles, hawks, and falcons soar high overhead. Woodpeckers with bright red heads peck on forest trees. Down below, wild turkeys waddle along the ground.

If you're quiet you might see a moose. But don't get too close!

THE SHOSHONE-BANNOCK INDIAN FESTIVAL

See the dancers in colorful beads and fringe. Watch the pony races and the Native American rodeo. You're enjoying the Shoshone-Bannock Indian Festival! It's on the Fort Hall **Reservation** near Blackfoot.

Many Native American groups live in Idaho. The Shoshone and Bannock are in the south. Their **ancestors** built cone-shaped homes of grass or bark. They caught fish, rabbits, and other small animals. They also hunted for antelope, bison, deer, and elk.

Several groups live in the north. The Nez Percé is one of the largest groups. Their ancestors lived in longhouses. They caught salmon and other fish.

Watch traditional Native American dances while in Idaho!

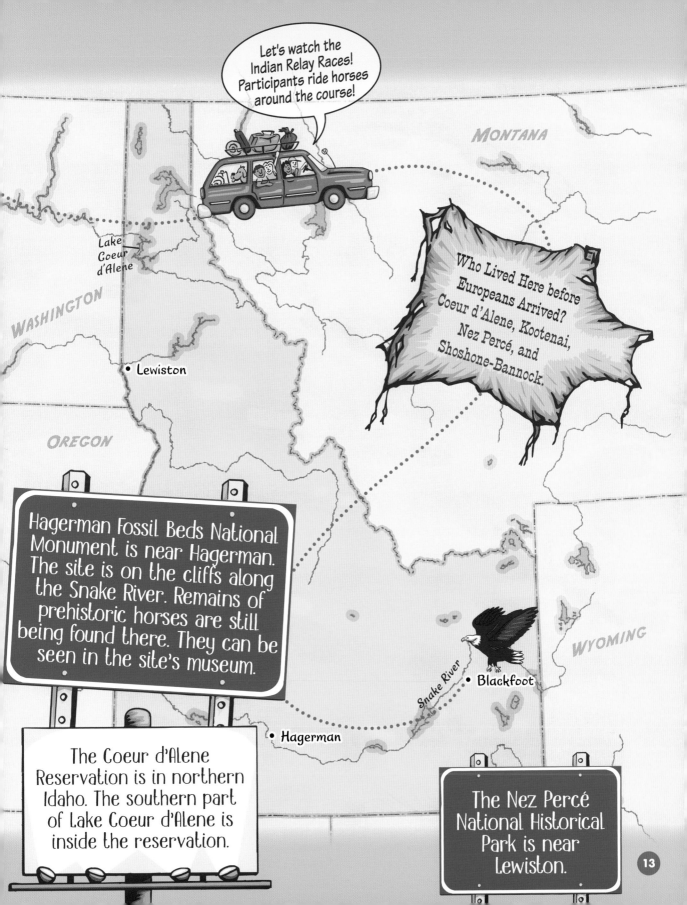

Let's watch the Indian Relay Races! Participants ride horses around the course!

MONTANA

Lake Coeur d'Alene

WASHINGTON

Lewiston

OREGON

Who Lived Here before Europeans Arrived? Coeur d'Alene, Kootenai, Nez Percé, and Shoshone-Bannock.

Hagerman Fossil Beds National Monument is near Hagerman. The site is on the cliffs along the Snake River. Remains of prehistoric horses are still being found there. They can be seen in the site's museum.

WYOMING

Snake River

Blackfoot

Hagerman

The Coeur d'Alene Reservation is in northern Idaho. The southern part of Lake Coeur d'Alene is inside the reservation.

The Nez Percé National Historical Park is near Lewiston.

SACAJAWEA'S BIRTHPLACE

Meriwether Lewis and William Clark explored present-day Idaho in 1805. They were the first white people in the area. They were exploring westward across North America. They hoped to reach the Pacific Ocean. The Shoshone and Nez Percé Native Americans helped the explorers.

A Shoshone woman joined them as a translator. Her name was Sacajawea. She could speak the local Native Americans' languages.

You'll learn all about Sacajawea in Salmon. Just visit the Sacajawea Interpretive, Cultural, and Education Center. It's in the Lemhi Valley, where Sacajawea was born. She came back to this place during her travels with Lewis and Clark.

The Outdoor School teaches visitors about life in Lemhi Valley in the 1800s.

OLD FORT HALL REPLICA IN POCATELLO

Stroll around Old Fort Hall Replica in Pocatello. This place has lots of memories. Weary trappers came here. Some were Native Americans, and some were white. They brought loads of animal furs for trade. They stocked up on supplies. Then they headed back out into the wilderness.

Fur traders set up many trading posts in Idaho. Fort Hall was built in 1834. Soon it became a welcome stop for pioneers. They were traveling west along the Oregon Trail.

Christian **missionaries** also came to Idaho. They built the Lapwai Mission in 1836. It stood near Lewiston. Mormons came to Idaho, too. In 1860, they settled in Franklin. That was Idaho's first permanent town.

Fur traders traveled along the Oregon Trail. They could rest at Old Fort Hall.

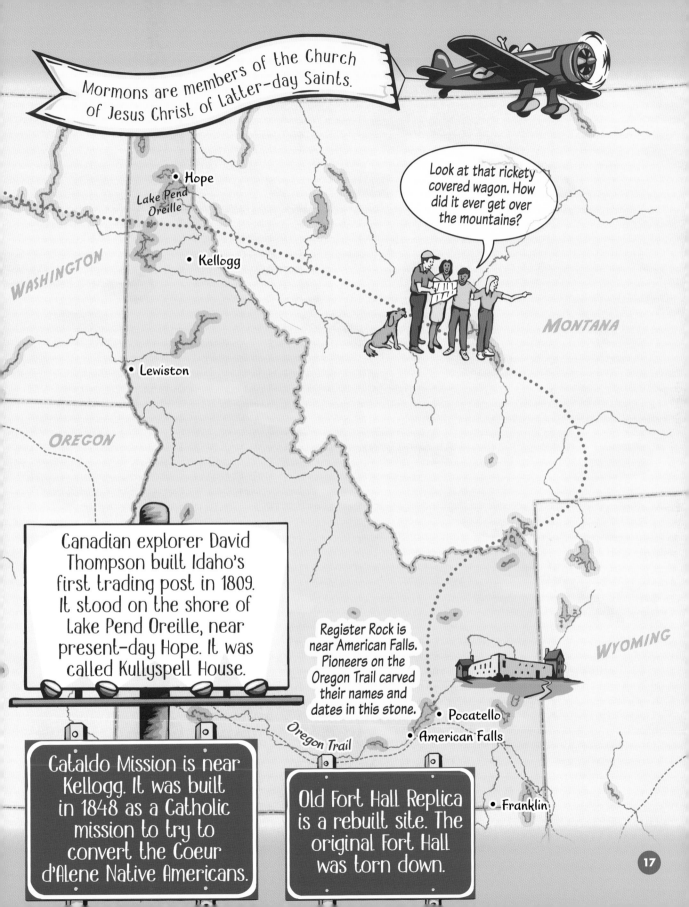

Mormons are members of the Church of Jesus Christ of Latter-day Saints.

Look at that rickety covered wagon. How did it ever get over the mountains?

Canadian explorer David Thompson built Idaho's first trading post in 1809. It stood on the shore of Lake Pend Oreille, near present-day Hope. It was called Kullyspell House.

Register Rock is near American Falls. Pioneers on the Oregon Trail carved their names and dates in this stone.

Cataldo Mission is near Kellogg. It was built in 1848 as a Catholic mission to try to convert the Coeur d'Alene Native Americans.

Old Fort Hall Replica is a rebuilt site. The original Fort Hall was torn down.

Hope
Lake Pend Oreille
Kellogg
Lewiston
WASHINGTON
OREGON
MONTANA
WYOMING
Oregon Trail
Pocatello
American Falls
Franklin

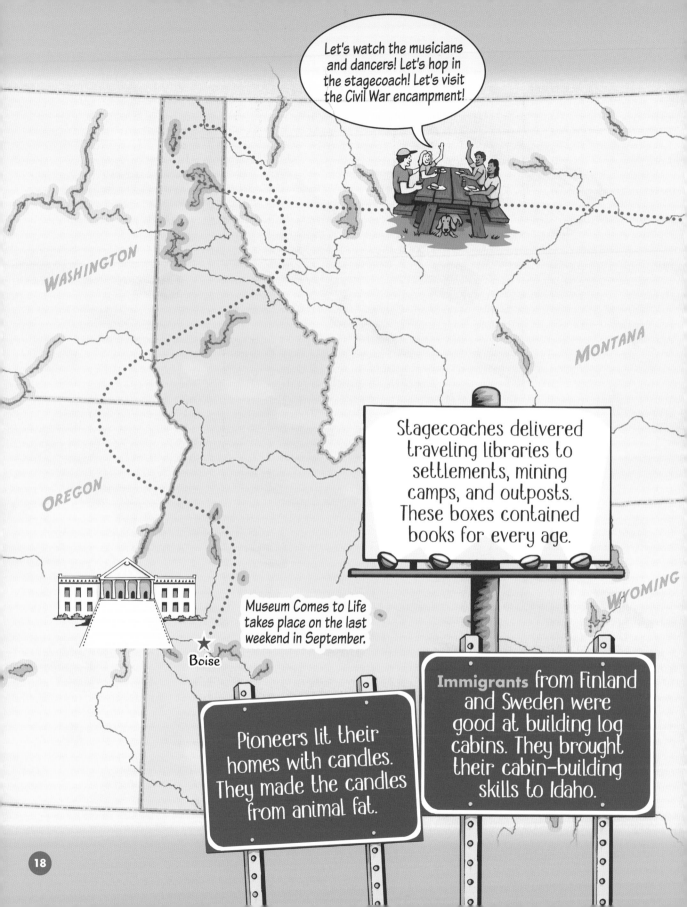

MUSEUM COMES TO LIFE

Watch mountain men build fires with **flint**. Enjoy some music in the saloon. Stroll through an old-time log cabin.

You're visiting Museum Comes to Life. It's a weekend festival that takes place in Boise every September. It's held in the city's Pioneer Village. At the village you'll learn about pioneer life. You'll also test your pioneer skills.

Pioneer life in Idaho was rough. People built log cabins and made their own clothes. They hunted deer and other animals for food. Winters could be bitterly cold. People snuggled under wool blankets or furs.

The festival also has music, dancing, war reenacting groups, crafts, and games. This living history event has been around for more than 40 years.

See reenactors of the Civil War and learn about Idaho's history!

BASQUES AND THE SAN INAZIO FESTIVAL

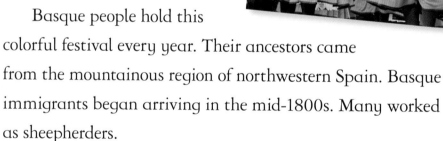

Kick-dancing boys kick higher than their heads. Girls in red skirts dance the hoop dance. Sheepherders' wagons stand around a square. It's the San Inazio Festival in Boise!

Basque people hold this colorful festival every year. Their ancestors came from the mountainous region of northwestern Spain. Basque immigrants began arriving in the mid-1800s. Many worked as sheepherders.

Much of Idaho is very lightly settled. Why? Because the land is so mountainous and rough. Most Idahoans live in two areas. One is the Snake River Plain. The other is between Lewiston and Coeur d'Alene.

Watch dancers in their bright clothing celebrate the San Inazio Festival.

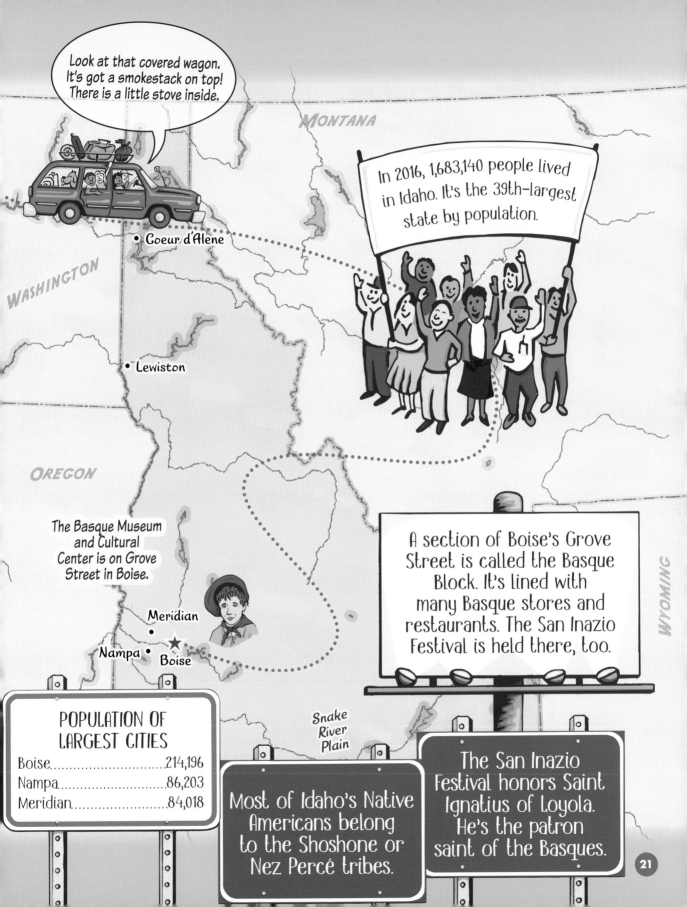

Look at that covered wagon. It's got a smokestack on top! There is a little stove inside.

MONTANA

In 2016, 1,683,140 people lived in Idaho. It's the 39th-largest state by population.

WASHINGTON

• Coeur d'Alene

• Lewiston

OREGON

The Basque Museum and Cultural Center is on Grove Street in Boise.

Meridian
•
Nampa • ★ Boise

A section of Boise's Grove Street is called the Basque Block. It's lined with many Basque stores and restaurants. The San Inazio Festival is held there, too.

WYOMING

Snake River Plain

POPULATION OF LARGEST CITIES
Boise.............................214,196
Nampa..............................86,203
Meridian............................84,018

Most of Idaho's Native Americans belong to the Shoshone or Nez Percé tribes.

The San Inazio Festival honors Saint Ignatius of Loyola. He's the patron saint of the Basques.

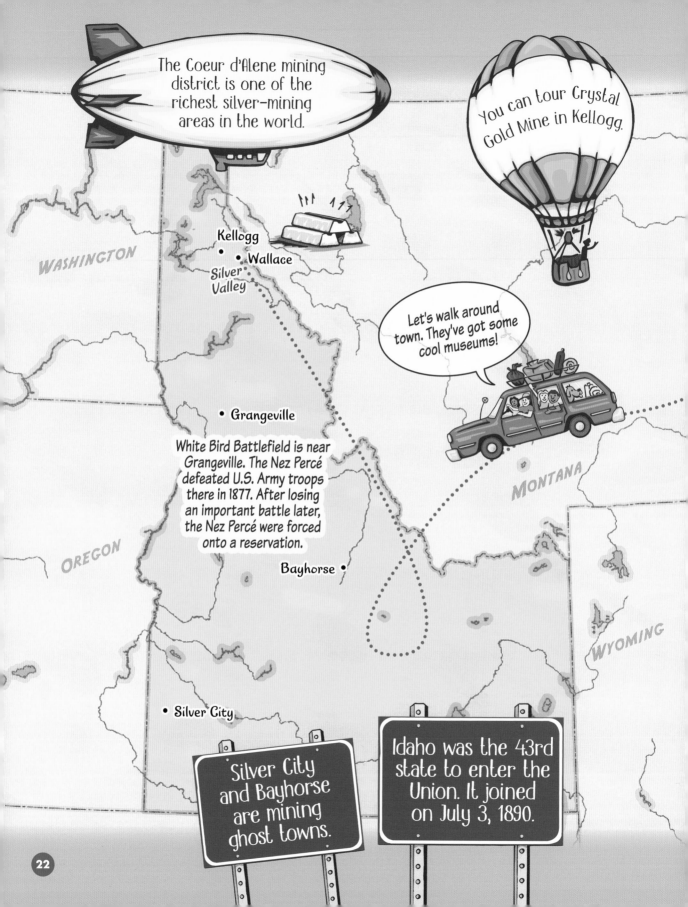

SIERRA SILVER MINE IN HISTORIC WALLACE

Put on your shiny yellow hard hat. Then head down into the silver mine. Your guide is a real miner. He shows how miners got the silver out.

You're touring Sierra Silver Mine. It's in the old mining town of Wallace.

Both silver and gold were discovered in Idaho. People found gold in 1860. Then silver was discovered in the 1870s. Wallace is in the Coeur d'Alene mining district. This region is often called Silver Valley.

Thousands of people rushed into Idaho once gold and silver were found there. They hoped to get rich. Some did, but most did not. The towns they left are now **ghost towns**.

Get ready to go underground and get a tour of the Sierra Silver Mine!

MINIDOKA DAM AND POWER PLANT NEAR RUPERT

Look at the area around Rupert. This land gets very little rain. Yet it has some of Idaho's richest farmland. What makes this happen? Minidoka Dam!

This dam is on the Snake River. It was completed in 1906. The dam holds back water, creating Lake Walcott. Water from the dam is directed through **canals**. From the canals, the water goes to farms. Near the dam is a power plant. It uses water power to create electricity.

Many other dams were built in Idaho. They are great for farmers. The dry land can now be used to grow lots of crops.

Minidoka Dam is 86 feet high (26 m) and was designed to manage the flow of the Snake River.

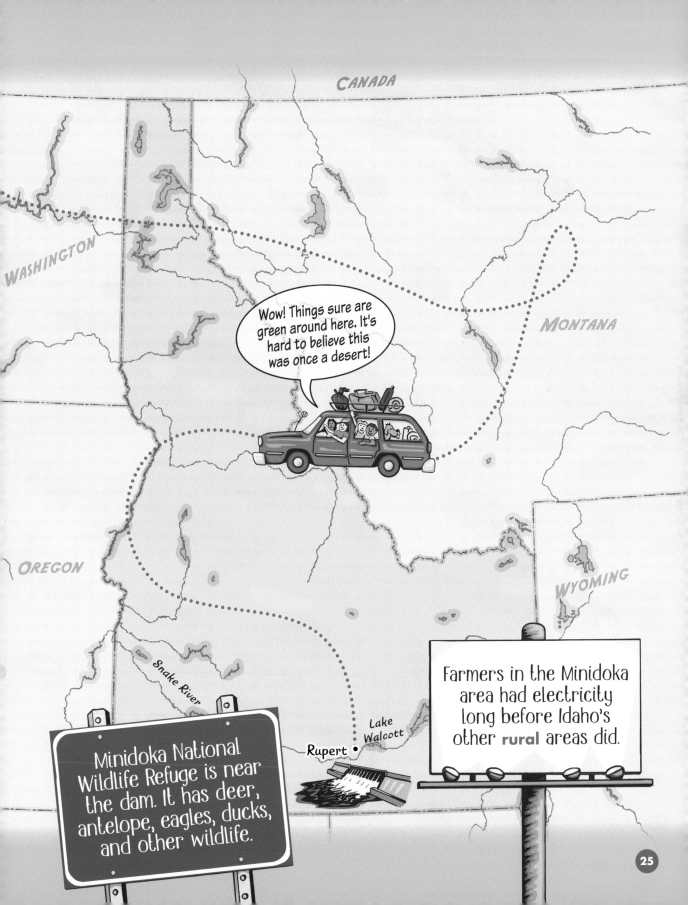

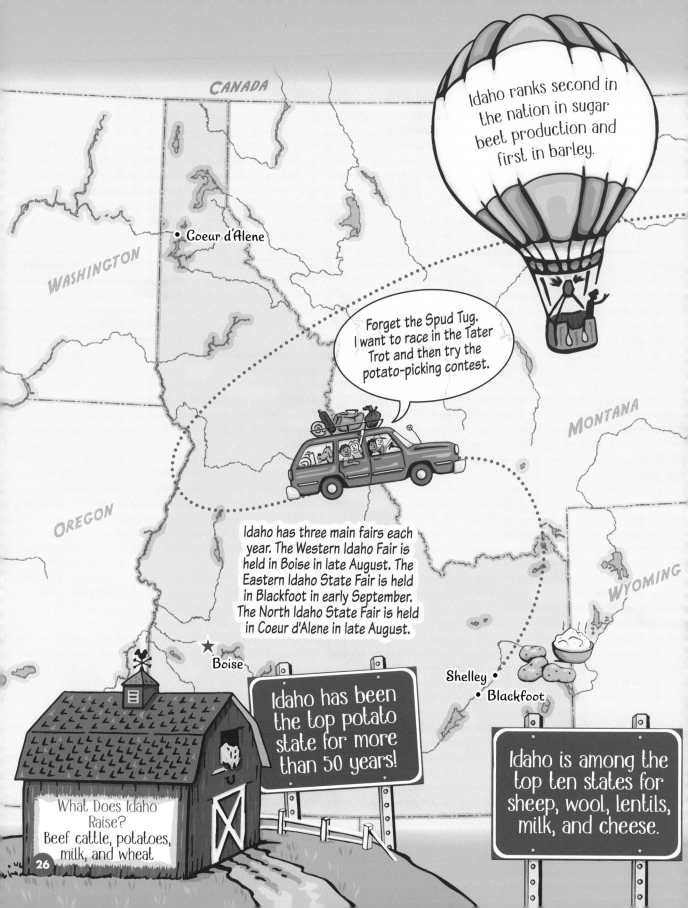

IDAHO SPUD DAY IN SHELLEY

Pull that rope, and don't let go. Splat! You lose! You've landed in a pit of mashed potatoes!

You're taking part in the big Spud Tug. This tug-of-war is messy but fun. It's just one event on Idaho Spud Day in Shelley.

Spud Day celebrates Idaho's number-one crop. That's potatoes! Their nickname is spuds. No other state grows more potatoes.

Beef cattle are Idaho's most valuable farm product. Many farmers raise dairy cattle, too. Sheep are another valuable farm animal. They provide both wool and meat.

Get ready for the annual Spud Tug!

THE IDAHO NATIONAL LABORATORY

You've probably never heard of Arco. Many scientists know about it, though. In 1955, a nearby power plant geared up. It switched on Arco's electricity.

Why is this a big deal? Because the electricity came from **nuclear** energy. Arco became the world's first nuclear-powered city. The experiment was a success. Now thousands of cities use nuclear power.

The power plant opened in 1949. Now it's the Idaho National Laboratory (INL). It's in Idaho Falls. You can visit parts of the center. You'll see where they switched on Arco's lights!

The Idaho National Laboratory conducts research on nuclear energy.

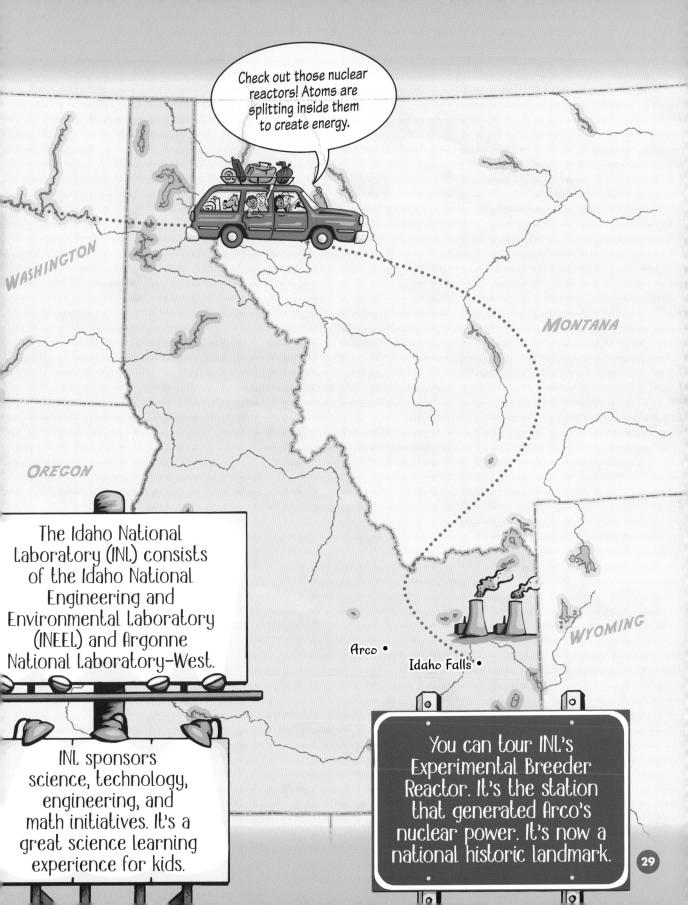

Check out those nuclear reactors! Atoms are splitting inside them to create energy.

WASHINGTON

MONTANA

OREGON

WYOMING

Arco •

Idaho Falls •

The Idaho National Laboratory (INL) consists of the Idaho National Engineering and Environmental Laboratory (INEEL) and Argonne National Laboratory-West.

INL sponsors science, technology, engineering, and math initiatives. It's a great science learning experience for kids.

You can tour INL's Experimental Breeder Reactor. It's the station that generated Arco's nuclear power. It's now a national historic landmark.

Hot water from deep underground is used to heat the capitol.

WASHINGTON

Look up on top of the dome! There's a copper eagle as big as a person!

MONTANA

OREGON

WYOMING

Boise

Idaho's state motto is "esto perpetua." This is Latin for "let it be perpetual."

Welcome to Boise, the capital of Idaho!

Four types of marble were used to make the capitol's walls and floors. They came from Alaska, Georgia, Vermont, and Italy.

THE STATE CAPITOL IN BOISE

Do you know anyone who's over 100 years old? The central part of Idaho's capitol building is. It was completed in 1912!

The capitol in Boise is a very important building. Inside are state government offices.

Idaho's state government has three branches. One branch has members from all over Idaho. They meet and make the state's laws. Another branch carries out the laws. It's headed by the governor. The third branch applies the laws. This branch is made up of judges. They decide whether someone has broken a law.

A copy of the Liberty Bell is outside the capitol building.

RIVER RAFTING IN IDAHO

Looking for a fun day in the sun? Then try river rafting down Idaho's Salmon River! Many cities along the Salmon River have local rafting businesses. They will take you on guided trips down the river. One company is in Stanley. Another is in Riggins.

You'll see whitewater rapids and rocky canyons that the river has carved throughout the years. Some areas of the river have wild rapids. Other parts of the river flow smoothly. The banks of the river have large, sand beaches if you need a break!

Wildlife is all around the Salmon River. Eagles, songbirds, and hawks fly above the river. Otters, mule deer, and bighorn sheep can occasionally be found at the river's sides. Don't forget to look for them during your rafting adventure.

Hold on tight! It can be a bumpy ride rafting down the Salmon River.

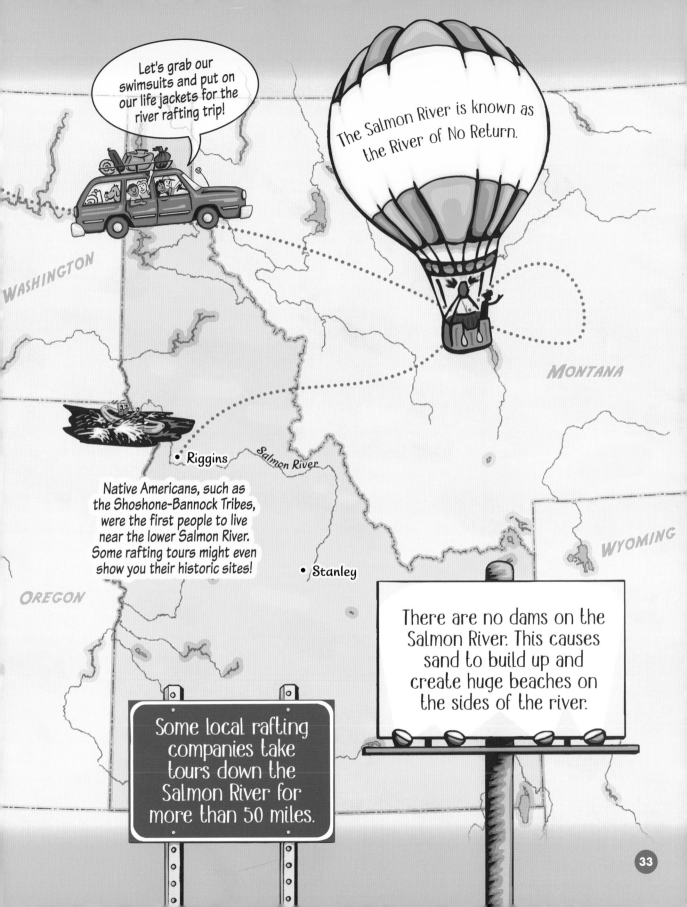

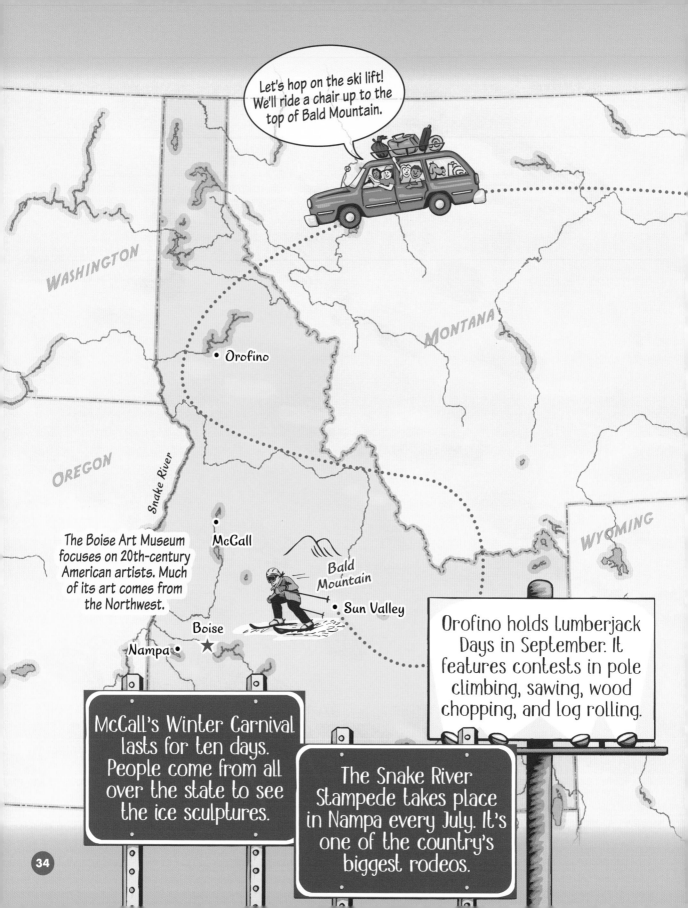

FUN IN SUN VALLEY

Do you like winter sports? Then head for Sun Valley. It's a popular spot for skiing. Even movie stars ski there! It's great for snowboarding and snowmobiling, too.

Skiing is a favorite sport in Idaho. So is ice-skating. Several cities hold winter carnivals. They feature ski races and other fun events.

There's plenty to do outdoors in Idaho. You can take wild boat rides through canyons. You can go horseback riding in the wilderness. You can fish, hike, and camp. Look around, and you see mountains and forests. No wonder visitors love Idaho!

There are always skiers on the slopes in Sun Valley during ski season!

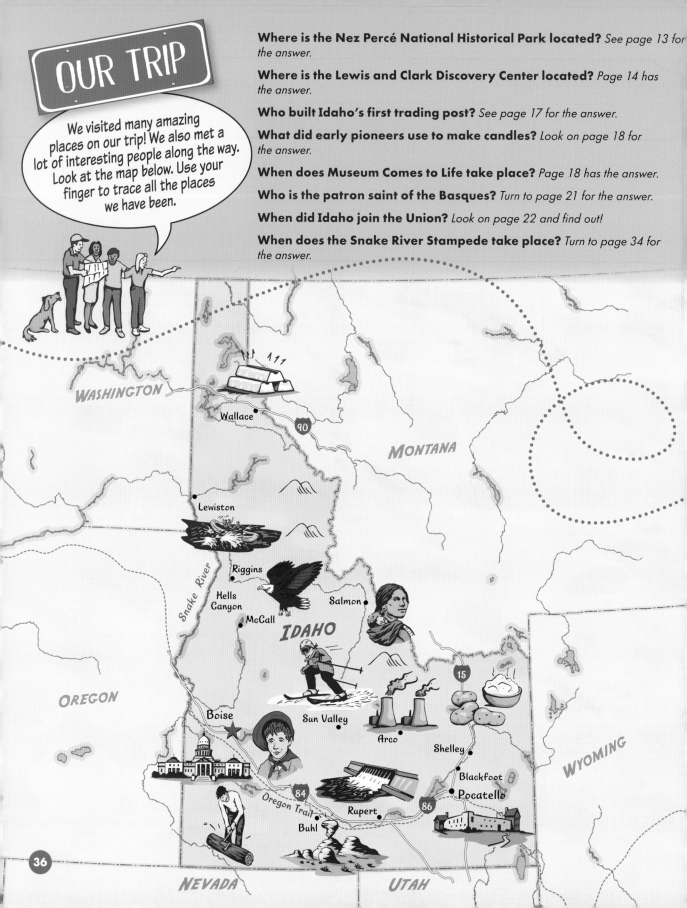

OUR TRIP

We visited many amazing places on our trip! We also met a lot of interesting people along the way. Look at the map below. Use your finger to trace all the places we have been.

Where is the Nez Percé National Historical Park located? *See page 13 for the answer.*

Where is the Lewis and Clark Discovery Center located? *Page 14 has the answer.*

Who built Idaho's first trading post? *See page 17 for the answer.*

What did early pioneers use to make candles? *Look on page 18 for the answer.*

When does Museum Comes to Life take place? *Page 18 has the answer.*

Who is the patron saint of the Basques? *Turn to page 21 for the answer.*

When did Idaho join the Union? *Look on page 22 and find out!*

When does the Snake River Stampede take place? *Turn to page 34 for the answer.*

WASHINGTON

Wallace

90

MONTANA

Lewiston

Riggins

Snake River

Hells Canyon

McCall

Salmon

IDAHO

Sun Valley

Arco

15

Shelley

Blackfoot

Pocatello

Boise

Oregon Trail

84

Rupert

86

Buhl

OREGON

WYOMING

NEVADA

UTAH

STATE SYMBOLS

State bird: Mountain bluebird

State fish: Cutthroat trout

State flower: Syringa

State folk dance: Square dance

State fossil: Hagerman horse fossil

State fruit: Huckleberry

State gemstone: Idaho star garnet

State horse: Appaloosa

State insect: Monarch butterfly

State tree: Western white pine

State vegetable: Potato

STATE SONG

"HERE WE HAVE IDAHO"

Words by Albert J. Tompkins and McKinley Helm, music by Sallie Hume-Douglas

You've heard of the wonders our land does possess,
Its beautiful valleys and hills.
The majestic forests where nature abounds,
We love every nook and rill.

Chorus:
And here we have Idaho,
Winning her way to fame.
Silver and gold in the sunlight blaze,
And romance lies in her name.

Singing, we're singing of you,
Ah, proudly too. All our lives thru,
We'll go singing, singing of you,
Singing of Idaho.

There's truly one state in this great land of ours,
Where ideals can be realized.
The pioneers made it so for you and me,
A legacy we'll always prize.

(Chorus)

State seal

That was a great trip! We have traveled all over Idaho! There are a few places that we didn't have time for, though. Next time, we plan to visit the Deer Flat National Wildlife Refuge near Nampa. If they're lucky, visitors can see everything from porcupines to bobcats. The refuge is also home to several types of birds and butterflies.

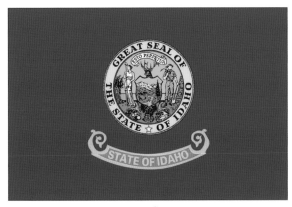

State flag

FAMOUS PEOPLE

Albertson, Joe (1906–1993), grocery chain founder

Bell, Terrel H. (1921–1996), educator and public official

Borglum, Gutzon (1867–1941), sculptor who created Mount Rushmore

Brink, Carol Ryrie (1895–1981), children's book author

Duke, Patty (1946–2016), actor

Farnsworth, Philo T. (1906–1971), inventor of the television

Fisher, Vardis (1895–1968), author

Hemingway, Ernest (1899–1961), author

Hemingway, Mariel (1961–), model and actor

Johnson, Walter (1887–1946), baseball player

Killebrew, Harmon (1936–2011), baseball player

Kramer, Jerry (1936–), football player

O'Brien, Dan (1966–), athlete and Olympic gold medalist

Palin, Sarah (1964–), American politician, former governor of Alaska, author

Pound, Ezra (1885–1972), poet

Sacajawea (ca. 1788–1812), Shoshone interpreter for the Lewis and Clark expedition

Simplot, J. R. (1909–2008), industrialist and billionaire

Spalding, Henry (ca. 1803–1874), missionary

Street, Picabo (1971–), skier and Olympic gold medalist

WORDS TO KNOW

ancestors (AN-sess-turz) parents, grandparents, great-grandparents, and so on

canals (kuh-NALZ) large ditches dug to bring water to fields

flint (FLINT) a hard rock that makes a spark when you strike two pieces together

ghost towns (GOHST TOUNZ) towns where no one lives anymore

gorge (GORJ) a deep valley with steep, rocky sides

immigrants (IM-uh-gruhnts) people who move into a new country

missionaries (MISH-uh-ner-eez) people who move somewhere to spread their religion

nuclear (NOO-klee-ur) having to do with energy produced by splitting atoms

reservation (rez-ur-VAY-shuhn) land set aside for a special use, such as for Native Americans

rural (RUR-uhl) in the countryside, away from cities and large towns

TO LEARN MORE

IN THE LIBRARY

Norwich, Grace. *I am Sacagawea*. New York, NY: Scholastic Inc., 2012.

Perish, Patrick. *Idaho: The Gem State*. Minneapolis, MN. Bellwether Media, 2014.

St. George, Judith. *What Was the Lewis and Clark Expedition?* New York, NY: Grosset & Dunlap, 2014.

Stanley, John. *Idaho: Past and Present*. New York, NY: Rosen Central, 2011.

ON THE WEB
Visit our Web site for links about Idaho:
childsworld.com/links

Note to Parents, Teachers, and Librarians: We routinely verify our Web links to make sure they are safe and active sites. So encourage your readers to check them out!

PLACES TO VISIT OR CONTACT
Visit Idaho
visitidaho.org
700 West State Street
PO Box 83720
Boise, ID 83720
208/334-2470
For more information about traveling in Idaho

Idaho State Historical Society
history.idaho.gov
214 Broadway Avenue
Boise, ID 83702
208/334-2120
For more information about the history of Idaho

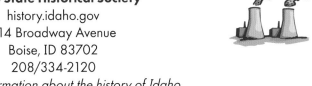

Idaho covers 83,569 square miles (216,443 sq km). It's the 14th-largest state in size.

INDEX

Bye, Gem State. We had a great time. We'll come back soon!